Don't Ever Cross That Road!

An Armadillo Story

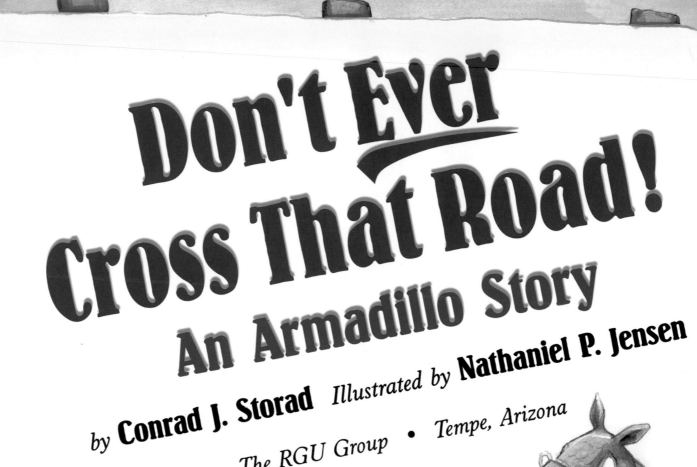

Don't Ever Cross That Road!

An Armadillo Story

by **Conrad J. Storad**   Illustrated by **Nathaniel P. Jensen**

The RGU Group • Tempe, Arizona

The illustrations were rendered in watercolor on Arches paper
The text type was set in Worcester
The display type was set in Bernhard and Springfield
Composed in the United States of America
Graphic layout by Julia C. Cabral and Adriana Patricia De La Roche
Production supervision by Denise Young

Printed in China

First impression

Library of Congress Catalog Number: 2003090521—Hardcover

International Standard Book Number: 1-891795-08-2—Hardcover

The RGU Group

www.theRGUgroup.com

10 9 8 7 6 5 4 3 2 (hc)

Once a teacher armadillo
Told his students gathered 'round,
"Listen close and hear my story,
And please do not make a sound.

My message is important
This is something you should know -
If you want a long and happy life
Don't EVER cross that road!

As rumbling cars and trucks zoom by,
You need to look both ways.
Bony skin is no protection -
One mistake can end your days!

Auto headlights in the darkest night
Draw bugs, a tempting treat -
Please remember teacher's warning:
Don't EVER cross that street!"

Then the teacher gave a lesson
'Dillos heard about their past.
Here's the armadillo's story -
You can learn it very fast.

Glyptodont

"Long ago the armadillos
Grew to more than ten feet long.
Like prehistoric army tanks
They lived, but now they're gone.

Today a 'dillo can be stout
Our armor shields us well!
Some say we look just like a pig
Stuffed in a turtle shell.

We have a small and narrow head,
A snout that forms our face,
Our hard skin, made of nine strong bands
Is called a carapace.

Our armadillo eyes are small,
Our ears are large and pointed,
Our bony tail has fourteen rings -
It looks as if it's jointed.

From snout to tip of bony tail
We're nearly three feet long.
We weigh as much as sixteen pounds -
Our digging feet are strong.

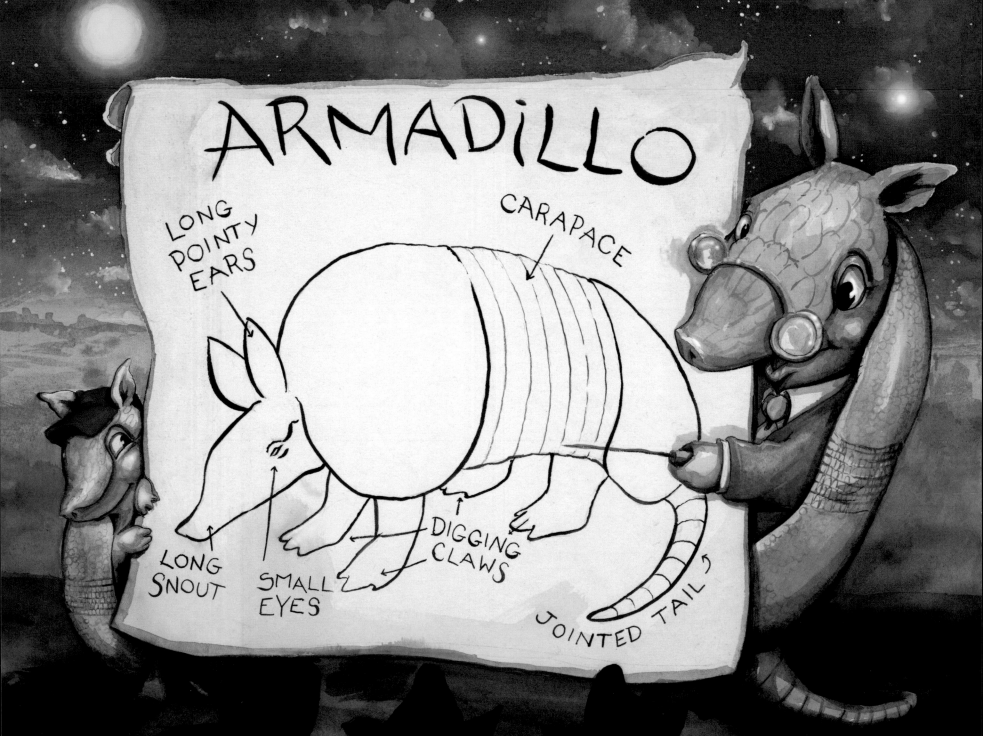

Armadillos can be very black,
Or brown or grayish-green.
We blend into the shadows
Where we cannot be seen.

Few animals can eat us,
And we never like to fight.
When predators are lurking
We run into the night.

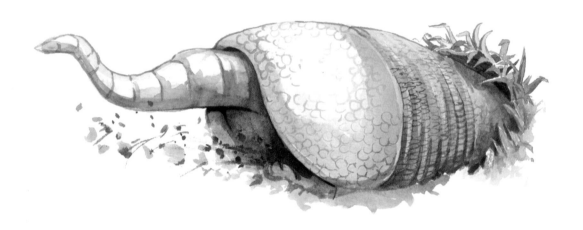

We hide inside a burrow
Or dig a new one fast.
We keep on digging deeper
'Til the scary danger's past.

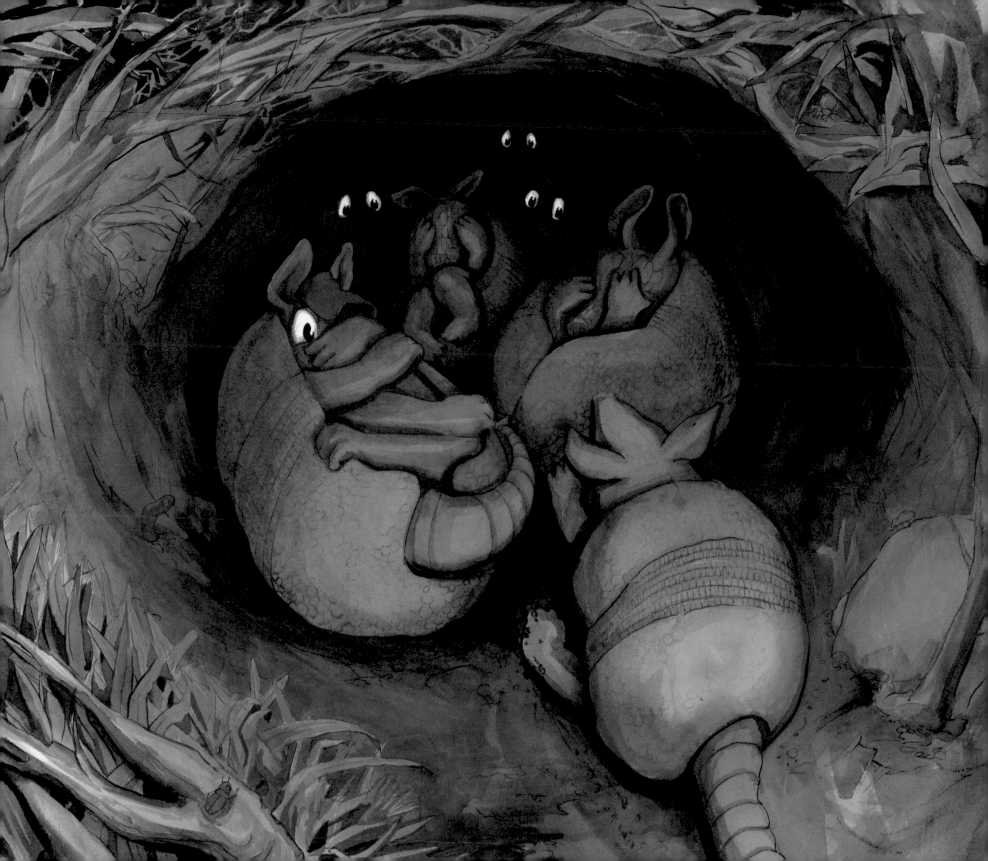

We make a funny grunting sound
And walk on strong, clawed feet.
We're hungry almost all the time
For yummy bugs to eat.

Our eyesight isn't very good,
And we don't hear that well,
But with our long and probing snout
Our sense of smell is swell!

We sniff for worms and beetles
When they're hiding underground,
And our special treat for dinner
Lives inside a termite mound.

With our tongue so long and sticky
We can swallow in one slurp
Sixty tasty little termites!
Fire ants don't make us burp.

Armadillos live near streams and woods.
We like the warm Southwest -
We mostly live in Texas
It's the place we love the best."

That ended teacher's lesson
But there's one last thing to know:
"If you want a long and happy life,
Don't EVER cross that road!"

Nine-banded or Long-nosed Armadillo
(*Dasypus novemcinctus*)

Weight: 10 to 16 pounds
Size: 1 to 3 feet from nose tip to tail tip
Diet: Ants, beetles, termites and other insects
Range: Throughout Texas; south and east through Louisiana, Mississippi, Alabama, Georgia, Florida and South Carolina; north and west into Arkansas, Missouri, Oklahoma and parts of Arizona and Colorado.

ARMADILLOS are strange-looking animals whose ancestors lived on the Earth more than 50 million years ago. The glyptodonts were huge armadillo-like creatures almost 10 feet long. They weighed nearly two tons. Today, most armadillos are not much bigger than a large house cat or small dog.

There are many different kinds of armadillos, but only one kind lives in North America. The nine-banded armadillo is found in the southern United States, Mexico, Central America, and parts of South America. It is sometimes called the long-nosed armadillo. In Texas, the nine-banded armadillo is the official state mammal.

The name "armadillo" comes from the Spanish word *armado*, and means "little armored one." Bony scales cover the animal's tiny head, narrow snout, short stubby legs, and long bony tail. John J. Audubon, a famous naturalist and artist who traveled throughout the United States in the early 1800s, wrote that the armadillo looked like a small pig stuffed into a turtle shell.

The armadillo's bony skin is called a carapace. It looks a bit like a turtle shell, but it is different in an important way. A turtle's shell is hard and immovable. The armadillo's carapace is flexible, which means it moves and bends as the animal walks along in search of food.

The armadillos found in the United States have nine bands of bony skin that surround their bodies and form the carapace. Between the bands the animal has skin and strong muscles. This hard skin is tough enough to protect the armadillo from predators – animals that would like to eat them.

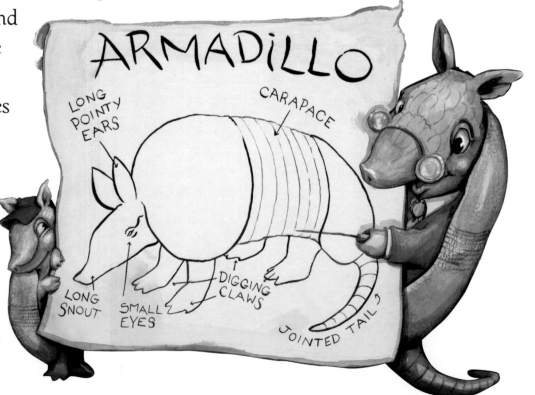

The armadillo does not have many enemies. It takes sharp teeth to crack an armadillo's armor! Most predators search for an easier meal. When in danger, the nine-banded armadillo will hunker down beneath its hard carapace. The armored skin protects the animal's soft parts from the teeth and claws of predators. In South America, another type of armadillo rolls up into a tight ball to protect itself.

Armadillos are shy, nocturnal creatures. Unlike most mammals, armadillos do not have fur. They lose lots of heat through their bony skin. As a result, they cannot survive in climates with long periods of cold weather.

Armadillos do not have sharp teeth for biting or chewing. Instead, they have 32 small, flat, peg-like teeth called molars. They use their molars to grind and crush food. The animals have very powerful legs. Each foot is equipped with strong, curved claws used for digging in the ground. Armadillos dig to find food, to make burrows where they live, and to escape from predators.

They use their long, sensitive snouts to sniff for insects and grub worms. Armadillos can smell food even when it is eight inches underground. The armadillo uses its sharp claws to dig up anthills and termite mounds. Nose down, it digs very fast when it gets a whiff of food. When digging, the armadillo holds its breath to avoid getting dirt and dust up its nose. It can hold its breath for up to six minutes.

Armadillos use their long, sticky tongues to slurp up insects, worms, and bug eggs. A hungry armadillo can catch 60 to 70 insects with one lick. A single meal might include 40,000 ants or termite grubs. Yummy!

What's for dessert? Some tasty, crunchy beetles would be perfect. But the armadillo must remember to be careful crossing the road to find them.

Some Words To Learn

armor: (AR-mohr) – A hard, protective body covering. Long ago, human soldiers used armor made from iron or steel to protect themselves in battle. An armadillo's hard, bony skin is natural armor. A turtle's shell is also a type of natural armor.

burrow: (BUR-oh) – A hole or tunnel in the ground dug by an armadillo or other animal for use as home, nest, or shelter.

carapace: (KAR-ah-payss) – Thick, protective skin that covers most of the armadillo's body. The armadillo's carapace does not cover its soft stomach. Turtles and tortoises also have a carapace, called a shell – so do beetles.

diurnal: (dye-UR-nuhl) – Active during the day. Diurnal creatures are active during the day and rest at night. Most humans and many types of birds are diurnal.

glyptodont: (GLIP-toh-dont) – A prehistoric ancestor of armadillos, anteaters, and sloths that lived in North and South America for millions of years. Some glyptodonts weighed nearly two tons. They became extinct around 10,000 years ago, during the last Ice Age.

nocturnal: (nok-TUR-nuhl) – Active at night. Nocturnal creatures are active at night and rest during the day. Scorpions, raccoons and many kinds of spiders are nocturnal.

predator: (PRED-a-tohr) – An animal that hunts and eats other animals.

snout: A long, projecting nose.

CONRAD J. STORAD grew up in Barberton, Ohio. He didn't see his first armadillo up close until 1982, when he drove across Texas on his way to begin graduate school at Arizona State University. Currently, Storad is the editor of the national award-winning ASU Research Magazine, and is the founding editor of Chain Reaction, a science magazine for young readers. He is also the author of *Don't Call Me Pig! A Javelina Story*; and *Lizards for Lunch, A Roadrunner's Tale*, as well as the creator of a number of science and nature books for children.

Recently, the Arizona Library Association and Libraries, Ltd. honored Storad with the Judy Goddard Award as their Children's Author of the Year. When he's not working, Conrad enjoys hiking and exploring the wilds of the Southwest with his wife Laurie.

NATHANIEL P. JENSEN grew up in Austin, Texas, attending Pflugerville Schools and obtaining a BFA from the University of Texas at Austin. Since 1990 he has been a working artist in Austin, where as a public artist he has painted murals as tall as 60 feet; as an illustrator he has created award-winning graphic illustrations for national, state and city publications; as a painter he has exhibited in venues large and small throughout the city; and as an art activist he has worked passionately to bring Austin arts to the forefront of community consciousness. This is his first book for children.